B O O K O F

EGGPLANT, OKRA & PEPPERS

NATIONAL
Gardening
ASSOCIATION

B O O K   O F

EGGPLANT, OKRA & PEPPERS

Edited by the staff of the
National Gardening magazine

I L L U S T R A T I O N S   B Y
E L A Y N E   S E A R S   &   L Y N   S E V E R A N C E

VILLARD BOOKS ▪ NEW YORK ▪ 1987

Library of Congress Catalogue
Card Number: 86-40342

ISBN 0-394-74990-1

Designed by Joel Avirom

Manufactured in the United States of America
9 8 7 6 5 4 3 2
Revised Edition

CONTENTS

EGGPLANT   1

OKRA   3

PEPPERS   6   Cells and Lobes—Two Different Words for the Same Thing
   7   Pepper Groups
   9   Chile, Chili, Cayenne, Jalapeño—By Any Name, It's HOT!
   10   Ornamental Peppers
   10   What Makes Peppers Hot?
   11   Can Anything Take the Hotness Out?

PICKING WHAT TO PLANT   12
   13   Seed Varieties

STARTING UP   17   Okra Seeds—A Tough Nut to Crack
   18   Some Basics on Starting from Seed Indoors
   20   Seedling Savvy
   21   Time to Repot
   21   Buying Transplants
   22   "Hardening Off" Transplants

WHERE WILL YOUR GARDEN GROW?   23   Vegetables in a Flower Bed
   24   No Land? Garden Anyway
   26   Container Plant Care

GARDEN PREP   27   Work the Soil
   27   Add Some Organic Matter
   28   Take a Soil Test
   28   Fertilizer

29 Anyone for Raised Beds?
30 A Pinch to Grow an Inch
30 Spacing

TRANSPLANTING 32

GROWING
34 Watch Out for Weeds
35 Weed Beater and More
36 Mulching Guide
40 Watering—A Little Dab Won't Do
41 Some Weather Words and Temperament Tips
42 A Little Something on the Side
43 Drip Line

WHAT'S BUGGING THEM?
45 Insect Control
46 Insect Problems
48 Disease Problems

HARVESTING
54 Stretching the Season
54 Up and In
56 Indoor Care
57 Bees Do It—But Only Outdoors

GENERAL COOKING TIPS
58 Eggplant
59 Okra
59 Peppers
60 Drying Peppers
61 The Spice Rack

FAVORITE RECIPES 62

FREEZING
82 Eggplant
82 Okra
83 Peppers

CANNING 84

B O O K   O F

EGGPLANT, OKRA & PEPPERS

EGGPLANT

Eggplant is the queen of the garden. Deep, almost purple-black in color, with a glossy sheen and a cap like a crown, it looks like royalty. Its taste is fit for royalty, too! Mouth-watering eggplant parmigiana, stuffed eggplant, or southern-style french-fried eggplant are always treats at the table.

Eggplant has been around a long time. It originally came from India and was introduced by Arabians to the people of Spain, who later brought it to this country. Both purple and white varieties were growing here by 1806.

One of the earliest references to eggplant is from a

fifth-century Chinese book. It seems that the Chinese ladies of that era considered it high fashion to stain their teeth with a black dye made from eggplant. They then polished their teeth until they shone like metal.

But eggplant, as a food or fashion accessory, wasn't always popular everywhere. In fifteenth- and sixteenth-century Europe, eggplants were called "mad apples," because it was thought that eating them would make a person insane. Even when this fear started dying away, Europeans still considered eggplant poisonous. Eggplant is a member of the nightshade family, the same as tomatoes, potatoes, tobacco, and belladonna. An eye-drop substance derived from belladonna (also called deadly nightshade) was once used by fashionable ladies to make their eyes appear larger. Once in a while, someone would drink belladonna and die of the effects. No wonder, knowing that eggplant and deadly nightshade were related, people shied away from eating eggplant. (Tomatoes, too, were taboo in certain areas.)

Eventually eggplant became as popular in Europe as it had been in the Middle East. In fact, it remains more popular in the Old World than it does here. There are more varieties under cultivation in Europe than there are in America, and Japan is now developing even more varieties.

The commercial production of eggplant in this country is mostly in Florida, but it is grown commercially on a small scale in many states, including California, New Jersey, Ohio, Colorado, Michigan, Illinois, Missouri, New York, and Texas. So you see, eggplant can be grown successfully almost everywhere. There's no reason you can't grow this pretty and tasty vegetable in your own home garden.

OKRA

Okra shines in the garden. It's a member of the hibiscus family. You've probably seen pictures of Hawaiian women with large hibiscus blossoms tucked behind their ears. Well, the blossoms on okra plants aren't quite as large and showy as those blossoms, but they are definitely one of the most beautiful blooms in the vegetable garden. They're ivory to creamy yellow in color, with a deep reddish-purple throat. They bloom for only a day. By sundown, the okra flower is wilted, whether or not it's been pollinated. If it is sunny—good bee-buzzing weather—you will see miniature okra pods underneath the wilted flowers. All the blooms on the okra plant won't be pollinated, but since plants blossom for a long time, you should get a sizable harvest.

Asia and Africa gave us okra. It grows wild in the upper

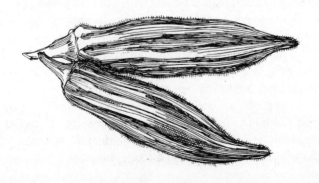

Nile region and was used in northern Africa for centuries. In fact, okra is an African word. Trading ships brought this vegetable to this country, and it quickly found favor as a crop and as an ingredient in French and Creole cooking in Louisiana.

Okra is a tasty and important ingredient in many foods, especially Creole dishes. Gumbo soup, a favorite in the southern part of the country, uses okra as a thickener. Okra is also often stewed with tomatoes, deep-fried, pickled, boiled, or steamed and served with butter. It can also be eaten raw, fresh from the garden. The gummy texture of okra doesn't appeal to everyone. Since this quality is more pronounced when it's boiled or steamed, okra seems to be most popular as an addition to soups and stews, fried, or pickled.

The seeds of okra can even be used as a coffee substitute. Let the pods ripen on the plant, collect the seeds when the ribs of the pods have opened, and roast and grind the seeds. The flavor of brewed okra is supposed to be similar to coffee, but without any bitterness. Another way to take advantage of okra's versatility is by grinding the dried seeds and using them to make bread, usually in combination with another meal, such as cornmeal.

Because it is easy to grow in hot climates, okra is one of those vegetables that's considered a "southern" crop. While it is true that the southern parts of our country have the long, hot growing seasons that okra needs to bear really well, it can still be grown anywhere.

Start plants early indoors in northern parts of the country. Yields in the shorter-season areas may not be as high as in longer-season climates, but gardeners can make up for that by simply growing a few extra plants.

PEPPERS

Peppers make the garden brighter for gardeners everywhere. The glistening greens of the leaves and the ripening peppers, the true scarlets and yellows of different varieties—all mark the rows where peppers are growing.

Besides their appearance, there's another reward from peppers. They're delicious. Sweet bell peppers go well with just about anything and are wonderful eaten right out of the garden, while the hotter varieties spice up many recipes. Some pepper varieties add color as well as flavor.

A strip of pimiento pepper can be stuffed into an olive, or deviled eggs can be sprinkled with a bright dash of paprika (paprika is made from peppers). Stuffed peppers, pickled peppers, fried peppers—peppers fit in, deliciously, everywhere.

Prehistoric remains in Peru show that peppers existed then, and we know that they were cultivated in Central and South America in very early times. Columbus brought them to Europe in 1493, and they were quickly adopted and cultivated. In fact, it was the Europeans that gave peppers their name. The only pepper they had known until that time was the black and white spice we still sprinkle out of our pepper shakers. When Columbus brought dried peppers back from the West Indies, Europeans said that this fruit was "hotter than the pepper of the Caucasus," the familiar table spice. The name "pepper" stuck, and we've been using it ever since.

In spite of the same name, our table pepper and the sweet and hot peppers we grow are not related. The black and white pepper we use are the seeds of the plant *Piper nigrum*, while our garden peppers belong to the genus *Capsicum*. *Capsicum annuum*, one species of the *Capsicum* genus, accounts for most of the varieties grown in this country. The exception is the Tabasco pepper, which belongs to another species, *Capsicum frutescens*.

Cells and Lobes—Two Different Words for the Same Thing

If you cut open a pepper crosswise near the stem, you'll notice thin walls that divide the pepper into sections. These sections are called "lobes," or "cells." Most seed companies describe a well-shaped sweet bell pepper as "blocky." The blocky shape comes from the division of the pepper into lobes, and a good blocky pepper will have three or four lobes. The shape of blocky peppers makes them great for stuffing, pepper rings, and general all-round use.

Pepper Groups

Seed companies break down the peppers we grow into two categories: hot and sweet. The "hot" include Cayenne, Celestial, and Large Cherry. Included in the "sweet" category are Bell, Banana, Pimiento, and Sweet Cherry.

BELL

These peppers are characterized by large, block-shaped fruits that have three or four lobes. They are usually about 3 inches wide, 4 inches long, and they taper slightly. Starting off as dark green to yellow-green, most turn red when fully ripe, although some turn yellow. They are often harvested and used when green. There are around two hundred varieties in the bell group. *California Wonder* and *Yolo Wonder* belong to this group.

PIMIENTO

These peppers are sweet and have very thick walls. The fruit is conical, 2 to 3 inches wide, 3 to 4 inches long, and slightly pointed. Pimientos are red when ripe, and they're most commonly used at this stage. Popular varieties include *Bighart*, *Truhart*, *Perfection*, and *Pimiento*.

CHERRY

These peppers are cherry or globe-shaped, with three

cells. They grow on long, upright stems, usually above the leaves of the plant. They are generally orange to deep red when harvested and may be sweet or hot, large or small. Varieties include *Bird's Eye*, *Red Cherry Small*, and *Red Cherry Large*.

CAYENNE

These are hot chile peppers. The fruit are slim, pointed, and slightly curved, ranging in length from 2 to 8 inches. Most of the fruit are green, ripening to red. They can be used in either the green or the red stage. Examples are *Anaheim* (a relatively mild pepper), *Cayenne*, *Serrano*, and *Jalapeño* varieties.

CELESTIAL

These very hot, cone-shaped peppers grow upright above the leaves of the plant. They're ¾ inch to 2 inches long, have three cells, and may or may not change color from yellowish to red or purplish to light orange-red. Different-colored fruits can appear on the same plant at the same time, which makes the plant very attractive. They're ornamental and grow best in containers—a wonderful patio plant. Popular varieties include *Floral Gem*, *Fresno Chile*, and *Celestial*.

TABASCO

These 1- to 3-inch-long fruits are slim, tapered, and *very* hot. They are attractive ornamental plants as well as having fruit that can be harvested. The most popular pepper of this group is *Tabasco*, which is grown commercially for making Tabasco sauce. Others are *Japanese Cluster*, *Coral Gem*, *Chili Piquin*, *Small Red Chili*, and very small *Cayenne*.

Chile, Chili, Cayenne, Jalapeño — By Any Name, It's HOT!

Names for hot peppers can get confusing. Some people call them chili peppers, some call them cayennes or jalapeños, and others just call them hot peppers. What are they really called? Is each of these names a separate category?

The confusion started in Mexico. "Chile" is Spanish for pepper. To specify which type of pepper, Mexicans would add the word for the particular type after the name *chile*. Therefore, *chile dulce* would be sweet pepper, *chile jalapeño* would be the jalapeño pepper, and so on. When *chile* found its way into this country, different meanings were given to it in various parts of the country, and it even acquired a new spelling. In the Southwest and West, *chile* is used to refer to the Anaheim pepper. In other parts of the South and Southeast and still other sections of the country, *chile* refers to any type of hot pepper. In still other parts of the United States, *chili* is the word for hot pepper. And all over the country we have the dishes chile and chili con carne, which are pepper based. Cayenne and Jalapeño are only two types of hot peppers; there are Anaheims, Serranos, and numerous others. *Chile* and *chili* are not varieties of peppers, but only words used to describe that the pepper is hot. So whether you say *chile* or *chili*, *cayenne* or *jalapeño*, and whether the word describes just an Anaheim pepper or all hot peppers, watch out! That pepper is HOT!

Ornamental Peppers

Ornamental peppers are members of the *Capsicum* genus like the peppers that are grown for food outdoors. Give them lots of sun and keep them evenly moist, and they'll produce many small cone-shaped peppers. These plants, which you can usually buy through a seed catalog, at a florist shop, or even in a supermarket, are very pretty when the miniature peppers start to ripen. Often you'll have a plant splashed with green, yellow, red, and orange all at the same time, since each pepper ripens at its own pace.

These mini-peppers are edible, but they are hot! You can use them in cooking or for attractive and different hors d'oeuvres along with crackers and a dip. Just be careful not to confuse them with a plant called the Jerusalem, or Christmas Cherry. Instead of the cone-shaped peppers, these plants have round fruit that is reddish-orange when ripe; they are not edible.

What Makes Peppers Hot?

Capsaicin, a substance present in most peppers, causes the hotness. Of course, it's present in much greater quantities in hot peppers, which makes them taste hotter than bell or sweet peppers. Capsaicin is so strong to the human taste bud that even a dilution of one part per million can be detected.

Where is the capsaicin? It's found in tiny, blisterlike sacs between the lining and the inner wall of the pepper. If you cut a pepper in half lengthwise, you will see the inside partitions that divide each pepper into lobes and surround the seed cavity. The clear membrane that covers these partitions also covers the blisterlike capsaicin sacs.

These sacs are easily broken if a pepper is handled at all roughly, releasing the capsaicin throughout the inside of the pepper and spreading the hotness.

Can Anything Take the Hotness Out?

Hot pepper seeds cause a burning sensation if they come into contact with your eyes or mouth, so always remove the stem and seed core when preparing them. You should wear rubber gloves when working with the extra-hot varieties, because the seeds and skins can burn your hands.

If you grow your own hot peppers and want to eat some fresh out of the garden, there is a way to take out some of the hotness.

Roll a fresh chile pepper between your hands, or roll it on the table as if you were rolling dough. This dislodges the seeds and breaks the capsaicin sacs. After rolling it for a while, take a razor blade or sharp knife and cut the pepper from near the stem end down to the bottom. Cut through only the wall of the pepper; don't cut the pepper into pieces. Repeat this cut in two other places. You now have a pepper that is in three sections, held together by the stem end. Holding it by the stem, dunk the pepper in a glass of water. After about thirty seconds to a minute of dunking, the pepper should be ready to eat. The water will wash out the seeds and a lot of the capsaicin. If the pepper is still too hot for your taste, dip it into a fresh glass of water for another minute or so. This will remove even more of the capsaicin.

In an Anaheim pepper, most of the capsaicin is contained near the stem end. Cutting off an inch of the pepper from the stem end makes for a milder-tasting Anaheim.

PICKING WHAT TO PLANT

*C*hoosing varieties of vegetables to plant is a most important step in planning your garden. Although the varieties listed below all have good points, so many new ones are introduced every year that a careful study of seed catalogs and packets before you choose will be time well spent. There are many factors to consider: days to maturity, yield, size of plant, disease resistance. Listed in the following chart are some of our favorite varieties of eggplant, okra, and peppers, as well as some newer varieties that we think are worth trying.

It is important to know that the days to maturity noted on the seed packet or in the catalog for peppers and eggplant is the number of days from the time you set your plants out in the garden; the days to maturity of okra is calculated from seed. It takes from six to ten weeks to grow an eggplant or pepper seedling sturdy enough for transplanting.

Eggplant, okra, and peppers are heat-loving plants. While some vegetables can tolerate a frost, these three won't stand for it. It's important that all danger of frost is past before you set these plants out in the garden. But how can you do that and still make sure they have enough time to produce a good crop before fall's first frost? Well, here's a way that's simple and almost foolproof. Call your local county extension service or the National Weather

Service and ask for the first and last average frost dates in your area. Then look at the days to maturity on seed packages, or in your garden catalog, for different varieties of eggplant, okra, and pepper. Choose varieties that will produce in the time you have available. You can also figure out if you have time for two plantings of these crops—some parts of the country do.

One other point before you start selecting seeds—there are so many different varieties of hot and sweet peppers (especially hot peppers), it would be very easy to write a whole book on pepper varieties alone! If you don't find what you are looking for on the list, check seed catalogs.

Seed Varieties

Variety	Days to Maturity from Transplants	Description
EGGPLANT		
Black Beauty	73–80	Dark, purplish-black fruits; round-to-globe-shaped fruits. Blunt and broad at blossom end when developed.
Burpee Hybrid	70	Tall with medium-sized, oval-to-round fruit. Highly drought- and disease-resistant.
Dusky	63	Early-maturing, oval fruits, glossy, very dark purplish-black. Medium sized.
Ichiban	61–65	Early maturing, oriental-style fruits (slender and long). Slow to develop seeds. Soft, dark-purple color. Heavy fruit set.

Variety	Days to Maturity from Transplants	Description
Black Bell	60–80	Round to oval fruits; deep purple-black. Prolific fruit set. Widely adapted.
Morden Midget	65	Medium-sized, deep-purple fruits. Small bushy plants, excellent for small garden or container growing.

OKRA

Variety	Days to Maturity from Transplants	Description
Clemson Spineless	56	Dark-green, slightly grooved pods. Pods are straight, pointed, and spineless.
Louisiana Green Velvet	60	Light-green, smooth, spineless pods. Tender.
White Velvet	60	Large, round white pods.
Spineless Green Velvet	58	Smooth, round, spineless pods, about ¾ inch in diameter.
Dwarf Green Long Pods	52–56	Ribbed, pointed fleshy pods. Dark-green color. Good for market or shipping.
Emerald	60	Dark-green, round, spineless pods.
Red Okra	60	Rich red color, reddish tint to plant. Grooved pods. Turns green when cooked.
Park's Candelabra Branching	50–60	Base-branching habit, with four to six bearing spikes per plant. Requires less growing space per yield than standard varieties. Pods are slightly rounded; lightly ribbed.

Variety	Days to Maturity from Transplants	Description
SWEET PEPPERS		
California Wonder	75	Green when young, red when ripe. Large, blocky shape with thick walls. Good for stuffing. Harvest when green or red.
Yolo Wonder	72–75	Green, turning to red when ripe. Big, blocky, three to four lobes. Harvest when green or red.
Golden Calwonder	75	Medium green to yellow, yellow when ripe. Medium-thick walls, three to four lobes. Harvest when green or yellow.
Bell Boy Hybrid	75	Medium-long, mostly four-lobed fruit. Green, maturing early to red. All-America winner. May be harvested when green or red.
Sweet Banana	72	Long, tapered fruits. Green changing to yellow and orange, red when ripe. Okay to harvest when orange, yellow, or red.
Hungarian Sweet Wax	65–70	Long, tapering fruit. Medium to thin walls; green to yellow, crimson when ripe. May be harvested as soon as fruit is large enough.
Sweet Cherry	78	Nearly round fruits about 1 to 1½ inches across. Red when ripe. Good for pickling whole. Best harvested when green or red.
HOT PEPPERS		
Anaheim M	77	Long, tapering fruit. Green turning bright red when ripe. Medium-thick walls, mildly hot.

Variety	Days to Maturity from Transplants	Description
Hungarian Wax	65	Bright yellow turning red; 6 to 8 inches long. Fairly hot. Harvest when red.
Long Cayenne	70–75	Finger-shaped, wrinkled, and twisted fruit; 5 inches long. Very hot. Harvest when red.
Jalapeño	65–75	Tapering, 3-inch fruits. Dark green maturing to red when ripe. Favorite for Mexican foods; very hot; ornamental. Harvest when red for storing.
Large Cherry	69	Slightly flattened globe fruits; 1½ inches across. Green turning red; hot. Harvest when red.

SWEET PIMIENTO PEPPERS

Variety	Days to Maturity from Transplants	Description
Truhart Pimiento	78	Heart-shaped; sweet; 3-inch fruits. Green maturing rapidly to red. Harvest when red.
Burpee's Early Pimiento	65	Heart-shaped; 3½ inches long; thick-walled fruits. Dark green turning bright red when ripe; smooth skin.
Pimiento Select	75	Small, smooth skin. Very mild. Green; red when ripe.

F ew gardeners sow their pepper or eggplant seeds directly into the ground. Most prefer either to buy transplants or to start their own seedlings indoors for outdoor planting when the weather and the ground has warmed enough.

Okra has a reputation for being hard to transplant, and since it doesn't require a very long season (about two months from seeding to first harvest), many gardeners sow their okra seeds right in the ground at the proper time. But if you want to and are willing to take a little extra care of the long tap or main root that okra develops, you can successfully transplant this crop.

Okra Seeds—A Tough Nut to Crack

Okra seeds have a very tough outer covering that makes it hard for them to sprout. Here's a little trick to make them germinate faster: Place your okra seeds in the freezer overnight. This makes the moisture in them expand and crack the outer covering. When you plant them the next day in the usual manner, they already have a good start toward germinating. Some gardeners soak the seeds for twenty-four hours. This, too, speeds germination by softening the outer covering. It takes a little longer than the freezer trick, but it also works well.

Some Basics on Starting from Seed Indoors

It's very easy to grow your own transplants, and growing your own gives you the freedom to pick your own varieties. It also lets you make sure the plants get the best care right from the very first seeds.

To grow your own transplants, all you need is:

1. Some sterilized soil or potting mix.
2. Suitable containers such as peat pots, flats, Jiffy 7's, milk cartons cut in half, or anything that will hold soil and provide proper drainage.
3. A place to put the seeds while they are germinating that will provide a warm, even temperature.
4. Plenty of sunshine or grow lights.
5. Seeds.

For good seed germination, make sure the container has holes for good drainage. If excess water can't drain, your seeds will rot.

All your efforts can be ruined by "damping off," a fungus disease that attacks the emerging seedlings if you don't take steps to prevent it. The best preventive measures are to make sure your potting soil mix is sterile and that you don't overwater.

Purchased soil and mixes are usually sterile. If you want to use your own garden soil, you can get rid of harmful fungus organisms and weed seeds by baking the soil in a shallow pan (such as a cookie sheet) in a 200°F oven for about an hour. Don't do this when you're hungry; the smell is enough to make you lose your appetite. And don't try to sterilize soil in a microwave oven—manufacturers say that it may damage the oven.

Garden soil should be mixed with peat moss, perlite, or vermiculite to improve drainage before sowing seeds. Use one-third to one-half of one or more of these soil amendments (by volume) to lighten the soil.

To start growing your transplants, fill the container with moistened (not wet) potting mix or soil. If you are using peat pots or Jiffy 7's, plant a few seeds in each. This ensures at least one good plant per pot. In flats, sprinkle the seeds about ¼ to ½ inch apart. Then firm them into the soil with a flat, rigid object such as a small wooden shingle or kitchen spatula. Sprinkle some more of the potting mix over the seeds, covering them to a depth of only two to four times their own diameter. For pepper and eggplant seeds, about ¼ inch of the moistened soil or mix is about right. Okra seeds are bigger and can take about an inch of covering. Firm the top of the soil again, so that the seeds come into good contact with the moistened soil to help germination.

Cover the flat or container with plastic wrap, or put it in a plastic bag to help retain moisture. Then place the bundle in a spot that is consistently warm but not hot, such as the top of the refrigerator. Cover the containers with a few sheets of newspaper to help insulate them.

A sunny window is the worst place to put seeds that are trying to germinate. It's the hottest place during the day and usually the coldest spot at night. These temperature extremes don't help the seeds to germinate. The top of your refrigerator is a good spot because the temperature is warm and constant, not to mention that it gets the flats or containers out of your way. Light is not important in germinating eggplant, okra, or pepper seeds. They don't need sunlight to sprout, just warmth and a bit of moisture.

Seedling Savvy

Start checking your seeds in a few days to see if they've sprouted. But be patient! Seeds don't usually sprout overnight, and okra may take longer than peppers or eggplant. Making sure the seeds receive consistent warmth will be the best thing you can do to help them sprout.

Once the seeds have sprouted, they'll need light. Remove the newspaper and plastic and put the containers in a sunny window or under fluorescent lights. If you are using lights, place the containers or flats a few inches below the tubes. As the plants grow, keep moving them so that the tops remain a few inches below the tubes. Too much distance between the plant and the lights will result in spindly, "leggy" plants. Plants need darkness, too, so make sure the lights are turned off for at least eight hours a night.

If the nights are still cold and you have placed your plants in a window, move them away from the window during the night. The chill won't help tender, young plants, and seedling leaves can be damaged if they come in contact with a very cold, frosty window.

Keep the soil moist but not wet. Water your seedlings gently, and use water at room temperature, if possible.

Fertilizing your plants is not necessary for a while, because they have enough nutrients stored in their seeds. Wait at least a week or two after they've sprouted to fertilize, or even until it's time to repot. Watch out for overfertilizing. Once you start, use a small amount of a water-soluble, balanced fertilizer once a week. This will encourage healthy, stocky growth.

Time to Repot

When your seedlings develop their second set of leaves, it's time to repot them into individual or bigger containers, such as large peat pots or milk cartons. You can even use a plastic dishpan for repotting. Poke some holes in the bottom of the pan, and put a layer of stones or gravel in the bottom to help with drainage. Using sterilized potting mix, fill the dishpan almost to the rim. You can mix about a teaspoon of plant food or fertilizer in with each gallon of soil; 5-10-10 is a suitable fertilizer to use.

Water the young plants well before you transplant. The wet soil will stick to the tender roots, protecting them during transplanting. Using a tablespoon or other small utensil, carefully lift the plants out of the flat one at a time.

Make a deep hole in the dishpan soil and set in the plant, about an inch deeper than it was in the flat. Leave 3 to 4 inches between the plants. Firm the soil around the plants and water gently. Fertilize them once a week using one-third the recommended dosage of water-soluble balanced fertilizer mixed with water.

Buying Transplants

If you can't or don't want to start your own transplants, you can usually buy them at a garden store, although the selection of seed varieties will not be as great as from seed catalogs. Healthy eggplant, okra, and pepper plants will be unblemished and will have a nice dark-green color.

Watch out for tall, spindly plants. Often, these plants didn't receive enough light when they were started. Blossoms on the plant are also a signal for "don't buy." A transplant's root system usually isn't strong enough to support flowers or fruit unless the plant is in a deep container. Also, check under leaves for aphids, whiteflies, and other insects—you want to buy a transplant, not future trouble!

Take time to choose the best, healthiest transplants. These are the plants that you'll be depending on for food. A little extra time being choosy will pay off in a healthy garden and a better harvest.

"Hardening Off" Transplants

One of the most important steps in planting comes before your plants get near the garden. This is the process known as "hardening off." Your plants have spent their short lives in a warm, protected place and need to get used to the outdoors gradually before they can be planted safely in your garden. Even your store-bought transplants usually need to be hardened off.

About ten days before you intend to plant, put your transplants outdoors in an area where they will be protected from direct sunlight and wind. Leave them out for a few hours and then bring them back inside. Repeat this each day, gradually increasing the amount of time they are outside and the intensity of light they're exposed to. After a week or so, leave the transplants out all day and all night. Of course, you should bring them indoors if there is any chance of a frost.

If you harden off your plants properly, they'll be strong and able to withstand full sun, breezes, and all the challenges they'll meet in the garden.

WHERE WILL YOUR GARDEN GROW?

While your plants are hardening off is the time to think about *where* you're going to grow them if you haven't already decided. Eggplant and peppers don't necessarily have to be planted in the vegetable garden. They can grow successfully in flower beds or in containers. Here's more information to help you decide where you want to grow these plants.

Sunshine is important for these heat-loving crops. When you plan your garden, put eggplant, okra, and peppers where they will receive the maximum amount of direct sunlight. Also be sure to place them in a well-drained area.

Vegetables in a Flower Bed

If you're mainly a flower gardener, you can still grow eggplant, okra, and peppers. Where? In a flower bed! Okra can be grown as a background plant, eggplant and peppers in with your other flowering plants. Their greenery, pretty flowers, and ripening fruit will complement your other plants and give you something to eat besides.

We've seen gardens with a long stretch of flowers and then some peppers and eggplant in between beds to provide some refreshing green between the masses of color—mighty pretty and mighty practical! Another place you can grow eggplant and peppers is between shrubs, providing the shrubs don't shade the plants too much.

So look around your yard and see where you can put some eggplant, okra, or peppers. We bet you'll find space you didn't think you had. Just be sure that you can pick your produce without damaging your other plants. Also, when growing vegetables in a flower bed, use only pesticides that are labeled for use on edible plants, even when spraying is directed at the ornamentals. Drift from dust or sprays intended for flowers can easily fall on nearby vegetable plants.

No Land? Garden Anyway

Some people would like to have a vegetable garden but don't have enough land; either they live in apartments and have no land, or have some other problem that makes them think they can't garden. Sometimes these people can find community gardening space in their city or town. But even if you can't find space, you can have a vegetable garden in containers. You can place containers on patios, porches, rooftops, or other locations and have a fresh vegetable harvest no matter where you live. Growing in containers is not only easy and productive, it can be decorative as well.

Peppers and eggplant are good container-gardening

MORE EXPERT ADVICE FROM THE NATIONAL GARDENING ASSOCIATION!

Try *National Gardening,* the colorful, practical magazine read by America's most successful gardeners. We'll send you your first issue *FREE!* If you like it, pay just $18 for 11 additional monthly issues. If you decide not to subscribe just write "cancel" on the bill, return it and owe nothing. Whatever you decide, the free issue is yours to keep and enjoy.

NAME _____

ADDRESS _____

CITY _____ STATE _____ ZIP _____

I've been gardening for:

0-1   1-3   3-5   5-10   10 + years

Age _____ .

E7FVLDN

BUSINESS REPLY MAIL

FIRST CLASS PERMIT NO. 17 BURLINGTON, VT.

POSTAGE WILL BE PAID BY ADDRESSEE

The National Gardening Association
Depot Square
Peterborough, NH 03458-9983

NO POSTAGE
NECESSARY
IF MAILED
IN THE
UNITED STATES

choices because of their relatively compact size and growing habits.

To get started, buy some plants at your local garden store or start plants indoors as you would for transplanting into an outdoor garden. You'll also need to buy some containers large enough to give the plants plenty of root room.

When your plants are ready for transplanting into a larger pot, harden them off as described earlier. It's easier to harden them off while they are still in their flats, or small pots. This saves you the trouble of moving a large, heavy pot in and out every day.

When the transplants are properly hardened off, it's time to move them into their permanent containers. There are lots of possibilities for containers—a large pot, a redwood tub, or even a bushel basket will do. No matter what type of container you choose, make sure it will hold about five gallons of potting mix per plant and that it has drainage holes. Some people who garden in containers like to have casters underneath their pots to make moving them easier. It's also a good idea if you have to move your potted plants around during the day to follow the sun.

You'll need some drainage material, such as stones, gravel, or clay pot shards (small broken pieces), a good potting mix or sterilized garden soil, and a place to put your potted plant where it will get the most sunlight. Place an inch or so of the drainage material in the bottom of the container, then fill it with the potting mix or soil, packing the soil very lightly. The soil line should be about an inch below the rim of the pot. When this is done, follow the same rules outlined for transplanting outdoors.

Container Plant Care

Mother Nature takes care of outdoor container plants pretty much the same way she takes care of plants in the garden. But since there is less soil available to container plants than there is to the garden-grown plants, they tend to dry out a bit sooner. Check your containers to make sure that the soil is kept moist but not wet, especially if your containers are on a balcony with a roof that prevents rain from watering the plant.

Fertilizing is no problem. A liquid fertilizer should be applied weekly. Fish emulsion, purchased from your garden store, or a complete water-soluble fertilizer may be used.

Even though your plants aren't out in the garden, they are still fair game for insects. Keep an eye on container plants for any signs of damage. If you find a pest, deal with it in the same way as those in the garden. Of course, if you are container-gardening on an apartment balcony, a patio, or similar place, you'll have to be extra-careful when using an insecticide, making sure that none of the dust or solution gets on surrounding surfaces, such as a barbecue grill or a child's toy. Certain homemade remedies, such as a soapy-water solution or a chile-powder-and-water solution may be a better answer to your problems.

GARDEN PREP

Work the Soil

In order to have good root development, which is important for the growth of the plant, the soil needs to be loose to a depth of 6 to 8 inches. You can use a tiller or a digging fork to break up the soil to this depth. Breaking up the soil helps roots develop and also uproots any weeds that are beginning to sprout.

Add Some Organic Matter

All types of soil can benefit from the addition of organic matter. It helps a light, sandy soil hold moisture and nutrients better, and wedges between the particles of heavy clay soils to help them drain better. Grass clippings, turned-under cover crops, leaves, compost, garden residues, or whatever you add that can decompose (with the help of millions of tiny bacteria already present in the soil) turn into the key ingredient of all good garden soil—humus.

LEAVES   MANURE   STRAW   PEAT MOSS

You'll also be feeding the earthworm, who helps aerate your soil by digging his tunnels and helps build up your soil's richness by adding his leftovers, "castings."

Take a Soil Test

Peppers and eggplant prefer a soil pH of about 5.5 to 6.8 (slightly acid). Okra also likes this pH range but is more tolerant of pH variations than eggplant and peppers.

A soil test will tell you if your soil is too "sweet," or alkaline, or whether it is too acid. Add lime to an acid soil and sulfur to alkaline soil to bring the pH level into the proper range.

You can test your garden soil for pH level with one of the soil test kits on the market today. Or your local county extension service will usually do it for you for a small fee.

Your extension agent will be able to tell you what amendments to make to bring the soil pH into the proper range, based on your soil test. The test done by the extension service will also tell you if any other nutrients are lacking in your soil, which brings us to the next garden preparation step.

Fertilizer

Eggplant, okra, and peppers are heavy feeders, but they are also picky eaters. They like small amounts of food all season long. Too much nitrogen will give you a beautiful foliage plant but won't give you much in the way of food. Before planting, add some organic fertilizer, such as dehydrated chicken manure, or any other type of animal manure. You also might work in a balanced fertilizer, such as 5-10-10, at the rate of two to four pounds per 100 square feet of soil. The numbers 5-10-10 refer to the percentages, by weight, of nitrogen (N), phosphorus (P), and potassium (K) in the bag of fertilizer. Work all this fertilizer into the soil, making sure it is covered. Be sure to cover it well, as your plants are liable to suffer from a hot foot, or burned roots, if they come into direct contact with the fertilizer. Giving someone a hot foot in a vaudeville show may have been funny, but giving one to your plants can be a killer.

Anyone for Raised Beds?

If your garden is too wet, either in certain sections or all over, consider making raised beds for your plants. Determine the width and length of the bed and walkways, using stakes for guidelines. Use a hoe to pull the soil from the walkways up onto the bed until there is a 4- to 8-inch difference between the height of the bed and the height of the walkway. After you've raised the soil and leveled off the bed, simply plant your transplants into the bed as you would in a conventional bed. The raised bed drains faster because excess water doesn't just sit there; it runs

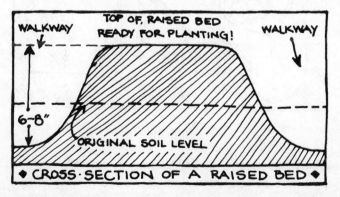

WALKWAY — TOP OF RAISED BED READY FOR PLANTING! — WALKWAY
6-8"
ORIGINAL SOIL LEVEL
◆ CROSS·SECTION OF A RAISED BED ◆

off. And having this water run off means your plants' roots will get the oxygen they need for good growth. An added bonus of raised beds is that they warm up faster in the spring and stay warmer all day long. This is a real help for plants such as eggplant, okra, and peppers.

A Pinch to Grow an Inch

When digging the holes for eggplant and pepper plants, give them the extra boost they need to get off to a good start by putting some fertilizer or compost in the bottom of the hole. Put a teaspoon of 5-10-10, mixed with some soil, into the bottom of the hole, and then cover that mixture with 1 to 2 inches of soil. The fertilizer should not come into direct contact with the roots because it can injure them. If you are using compost, a handful in the bottom of the hole gives plants that extra boost for needed quick healthy root development.

Spacing

When you're ready to transplant peppers and eggplant, dig a hole for each plant about 6 to 8 inches deep. Space two holes about 10 to 15 inches apart, then move down the row about 10 to 15 inches and dig another hole in that row between the first two holes. The rows will have a diamond pattern, with about 10 to 15 inches between each plant on all sides. You can get more produce from the space available by planting this way, but the peppers and eggplant are still far enough apart for good, thick foliage to develop. Good foliage is important to protect the fruit and help prevent sunscald. Pimiento peppers need a bit more growing room than bell peppers.

If you want to space your plants in single rows, set them one behind the other with about 10 to 15 inches between plants and about 2 feet between rows. Adjust the width of your rows depending on the way you cultivate your plants. If you cultivate with a hoe or other hand tool, your rows can be a bit closer together. One to 2 feet will give you enough room so you and the plants don't feel crowded.

Okra is easily grown from seed started right in the garden. Just stake out the length of the row, then dig a shallow furrow with a hoe in the prepared seedbed. Drop a seed every 3 to 4 inches of soil. About 100 feet of row can be planted with 1 ounce of okra seed. After covering the seed, firm the soil with the back of the hoe, so that the seed makes good contact with the soil. Once you've finished planting, water the soil gently if it's dry. This will firm the soil around the seeds and also prevent them from drying out.

When the new okra plants are about 3 to 4 inches high, thin them to their proper spacing—12 to 15 inches between plants.

TRANSPLANTING

Transplanting is a major step that can make or break your crop. However, it doesn't have to be traumatic to your plants if you have thoroughly prepared the soil, hardened off the plants well, and if you keep these few basic principles in mind.

Transplant on a cloudy day. Bright sun can hurt newly planted seedlings, so always plan to transplant on an overcast day, in late afternoon or in the evening.

Early planting. Generally, set out your plants the week after the last average frost date to be sure the tender young plants don't suffer from frostbite. To get a jump on the season, you can plant around the last average frost date (perhaps even two weeks before), depending on how warm the weather has been. When you plant early and frost is expected, protect your plants with hotcaps or cloches, either store-bought or homemade of newspaper or wax paper.

Another trick to keep Jack Frost at bay and increase the heat around these plants is to make a ring of black roofing paper about 5 to 6 inches high and 6 to 8 inches in diameter. Place it so the plant is in the center of the circle. The black paper absorbs and holds the sun's heat, increasing the temperature in the area around the plant. It really seems to help the growth of eggplant, okra, and peppers.

Plants need a soak. If you water your plants well, about an hour before transplanting, the soil will stay firmly around the roots to protect them, and make them easier to handle while putting them in the ground. The soil should clump together without being muddy.

Head off cutworms. One of the simplest treatments to prevent cutworm damage can be done when you transplant. Simply take a strip of newspaper about 2 or 3 inches wide and wrap it around the stem of the plant. When you place the plant in its hole, make sure that the newspaper strip is below ground surface for a depth of about 1 inch and that the rest is aboveground. This prevents the cutworm from chewing through the stem of your tender, young plant.

Work quickly. Even though you've hardened off your transplants, they still have tender roots. Getting them into the ground quickly will help prevent any damage to the roots and help minimize the shock.

GROWING

Now that your seeds and plants are in the ground, the true joy of gardening begins: caring for them so that they'll produce beautiful, luscious vegetables.

Watch Out for Weeds

Weeds will compete with plants for the same space, sun, water, and nutrients. So make it a practice to go out there and cultivate. Regular cultivation keeps the weeds down and makes sure the plants get all the water and nutrients available.

It's important to remember that whether you cultivate with a hoe, tiller, iron garden rake, or other weed-beating tool, cultivation should be shallow—not more than 1 inch below the surface of the soil. Weed seeds are usually close to the surface, and deep cultivation will only bring more of them up near the surface, where they can germinate. If you cultivate too deeply, you may injure the roots of your plants.

The best time to weed is after a rain when the plants have dried off, but before the soil has dried out completely. Get those weeds before they get a good start, and they'll pull easily from loose, moist soil.

Weed Beater and More

A good way to beat weeds is to mulch your plants. A thick mulch stops weeds from germinating by preventing sunlight from coming through. Mulch also keeps moisture in the soil, so your plants won't dry out as quickly. Many southern gardeners use thick mulches of hay, straw, or other materials to protect the roots of their eggplant and pepper plants from too much heat in the summer months. Mulch two to three weeks after planting to allow soil to warm up.

The following chart will help you decide which mulching materials to use.

Mulching Guide

Material	Type*	Thickness Used to Control Weeds
Aluminum foil or foil-backed paper	WND	one layer
Compost	D	1–2 inches
Cottonseed hulls	D	2–4 inches
Grass clippings	D	2–3 inchess
Hay	D	6–8 inches

*D—decomposes.
 WND—will not decompose.

Advantages	Disadvantages	Special Comments
Good for shady gardens as it increases the light around the plants; aphids and other insects avoid foil mulched plants; can be used more than once.	Foil can tear if handled roughly; can be expensive; can be considered artificial-looking.	Keeps ground very cool so better for midsummer than spring. Apply only after ground has warmed up.
Good feeding mulch; partially decomposed compost will continue decomposition quickly into humus.	Must have had sufficient heating period to kill any weed seeds and bacteria or diseases; may have unpleasant odor.	Plan and start ahead so compost will be ready when you need it.
Readily available in areas of the South, have a fertilizer value similar to cottonseed meal.	Very light, so wind can scatter.	For weed control sift between plants in multiple rows; can be covered with a very thin layer of other mulch to prevent scattering by wind.
Improves soil by adding organic matter; readily available almost everywhere.	Absorbent; may carry weed seeds.	May be mixed with other materials to prevent packing down; bottom layer may decompose rapidly so additional layers needed. Should be dried for a few days after cutting to prevent rotting.
Obtainable in large quantities; legume hays, such as alfalfa, add large amounts of nitrogen to soil.	First cut hay usually full of weed seeds not always attractive; not best for weed control.	Second or third cut hay more likely to be free of weed seeds; chopped hay may be more attractive. May not have to add more during season—just fluff up what is there.

Leaves	D	2–3 inches
Peat moss	D	1–2 inches
Pine needles	D	3–4 inches
Polyethylene (black plastic)	WND	One layer
Salt marsh hay	D	4–6 inches
Seaweed	D	3–4 inches
Straw	D	6–8 inches

Readily available to most people; contain many trace minerals; best food for earthworms.	May become soggy and pack down, becoming hard for water to penetrate to soil. Best to compost leaves first; else may inhibit germination.	Chopping will prevent packing down or matting. Mixing with other mulch materials will also prevent this.
Clean and free of weed seeds.	Extremely absorbent so water will not readily penetrate to soil; can be expensive. Adds little or no nutrients to soil.	Very good as soil conditioner; loosens heavy soil; improves water retention on sandy soil. Acidic; long decomposition time.
Light; usually free of weed seeds; absorbs little moisture. Can be reused; does not pack down.	Decomposes very slowly; sometimes earthworm activity beneath them.	Add extra nitrogen fertilizer if faster decomposition is wanted; slightly acidic in nature.
Can be reused; free of weed seeds; absorbs no moisture. Effective weed control, even with perennial weeds.	Hard to apply properly. Is not penetrable so rain cannot easily get through; may make soil too warm; unattractive.	Warm soil in spring; effective with warmth-loving crops. Ground must be moist before applying. Adds nothing to soil.
Usually weed-free; free and easy to gather in marshy areas or along marshy coast. Long-lasting and can be reused.	Not available to everyone; expensive if purchased.	Can be tilled under at end of season, chopping may make more attractive and easier to handle; does not decompose rapidly.
Can be used more than once; available at little cost or free to those along coast; water penetrates to soil easily.	Not readily available inland unless sold (packaged) at store; may have excess salt content; not necessarily attractive.	Salt can be washed out if left outside in a number of rains or hosed often or soaked in water with water changed often. Decomposes slowly.
Readily available in some areas.	One of the best mulching materials. Often difficult to obtain and handle; can be a fire hazard.	Chopping may make more attractive and easier to handle.

Watering—A Little Dab Won't Do

For healthy and rapid growth, your plants need about an inch of water per week. A rain gauge can be used to measure the amount of rainfall. You can buy a gauge in a garden supply store or from a seed and garden supply catalog, or you can make a simple one from a tin can with measurements scratched on the side.

Check the gauge often, and if Mother Nature hasn't supplied enough water, get out there and water. It's easiest to let your sprinkler do the work if you have a large garden, but if your garden is small, a hose or even a watering can will do the trick as long as you make sure the plants are getting 1 inch of water each week.

If you use a sprinkler, place tin cans in different parts of the garden. Check the amount of water that collects in them as you sprinkle, and keep track of the amount of time it takes for the water to collect. Move the sprinkler when the amount of water in the can getting the greatest amount measures an inch. When you move the sprinkler, overlap the areas being watered. This simply means moving the sprinkler so that part of the spray falls on the area you have just watered that received less than an inch. When an area has received a total of an inch, move the sprinkler, overlapping areas again. After you have watered and measured in this way a few times, you'll have a good idea how long your sprinkler needs to run in different areas of your garden so that the entire garden gets just the right amount of water.

Eggplant, although it has the same need for water as peppers and okra, is a fairly drought-resistant plant.

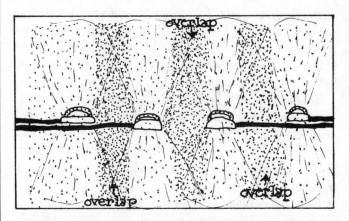

Be careful not to overwater your okra. Not only does overwatering cut off the vital supply of oxygen to the roots of all your plants, it also causes okra to produce too much foliage and not enough okra pods.

Some Weather Words and Temperament Tips

As any good gardener knows, a lot of variables go into producing a good crop of any vegetable. Just like any other plants, eggplant, okra, and peppers have their likes and dislikes as far as good growing conditions are concerned. One of their biggest likes is warmth, and one of their dislikes is cool nights.

Peppers and eggplant are fussiest right around blossom time. They'll have a poor fruit set if temperatures at night are below 55°F or above 75°F while they are blossoming, and they'll also drop their blossoms if daytime temperatures are above 90°F. These temperatures will also delay the fruit that does manage to set. Eggplant and peppers, too, can become stunted during cool weather and then not grow rapidly once warm weather returns. Rapid growth is necessary for quality fruit production. It's also interesting to know that large-fruited eggplant are more demanding than small-fruited varieties. So, if you've had a difficult time in the past growing eggplant, settle for the more succulent, smaller varieties.

There is not much a gardener can do about hot weather, but covering plants with cardboard boxes at night may keep in the day's heat if you expect a cool night. Using the circle of black roofing paper mentioned earlier or individual plant covers may also help if the weather turns cool.

Okra blossoms last only a day whether or not they're pollinated. Constant rainy weather when they're blooming can reduce yields, since bees don't buzz around much when it's raining. Despite these preferences, healthy plants will produce enough blossoms to endure a spell of bad weather and still produce fruit.

A Little Something on the Side

Eggplant, okra, and peppers are fairly big eaters, but they don't like their nourishment all in one dose. Sidedress them a few times during the growing season. Sidedressing is working a small amount of fertilizer into the soil 3 inches from the plants' stems to provide them with a steady diet. It's very easy to do, and the reward is a good crop.

Use an organic fertilizer such as dried manure or cottonseed meal, or a balanced commercial fertilizer such as 5-10-10. When you are selecting fertilizer for these crops, be sure that it doesn't contain too much nitrogen. The lush foliage nitrogen encourages is great for plants such as lettuce, but when other plants are putting their energy into making greenery, they're not making fruit. It's better to have the food on the table!

Eggplants, okra, and peppers should get their first side-dressing around blossom time, usually a month after they have been put outside. Sidedress them again about a month later, after the first fruits have developed. This helps them keep producing by giving them a little extra boost after all that work.

Drip Line

When rain or water falls onto a plant, it will drip off the leaves. The circle on the ground made by the rain dripping

off the outermost leaves of the plant is called the drip line. The diameter of this drip line varies with the size of the plant: the bushier the plant, the bigger the drip line. You can also figure out the drip line by the shadow cast by a plant. When the sun is right above the plant, look at the shadow on the ground cast by the leaves. The outer rim of the shadow will be about the same as the drip line.

To sidedress, just dig a trench around the plant about 1 inch deep and about 3 to 4 inches away from the stem around the drip line of the leaves. Put about a handful of manure or compost or two to three Tablespoons of 5-10-10 fertilizer in a band in the trench. Cover the fertilizer with soil. If the plants are in rows, dig a shallow trench one inch deep along either side of the row, again at the drip line of the leaves. Then sprinkle a band of balanced fertilizer in the trench, using about ½ cup of 5-10-10 per 10 feet of row, or a layer of manure about 1 inch deep along the length of the row. Cover that with soil, too.

No matter whether you use the circular-trench or row-trench method, be careful not to sprinkle any fertilizer on the plants, as it will burn them. Next, water the soil to send the fertilizer down to the roots.

Be careful not to overfertilize when you're doing sidedressing. That's probably the most common mistake that people make with eggplant, okra, and peppers. Sidedress properly, and you should be rewarded with healthy plants and lots of produce.

WHAT'S BUGGING THEM?

Insect Control

Some folks prefer using homemade remedies for insect control as opposed to chemical remedies. These homemade bug chasers include a soapy-water solution for aphids and a chile-powder-and-water mixture for other pests. Or if you find small groups of insects starting to chew on your plants, you can often pick them off before they've done any real harm. Keep your garden clean of debris, so that insects won't have a place to reproduce.

For some insect problems, gardeners may choose to use commercially available pesticides for controls. Be extremely careful when using commercial insecticides. There are some things to keep in mind when controlling insects in the garden.

Some chemical products, including Carbaryl, are harmful to bees. If you use them, do so near evening, after the bees have finished gathering for the day. Decreased bee activity will reduce pollination in your garden.

Check the label on any commercial product to find out if there is a waiting period between use and harvest. Read the label three times: when you buy the product, when you use it, and before you put it away.

Pay attention to the timing and the life cycle of the insect you're dealing with. If you catch the problem early—before the adults have laid eggs and hundreds or thousands of new insects emerge—you'll need less control and there'll be less damage to the crops.

Since pesticides come under a safety review on a regular basis, and since new pesticides are continually brought on the market, we recommend that you check with your local county extension agent about the latest commercially available controls that are safe and effective for home garden use.

Insect Problems

In the North, there aren't too many problems with insects bothering eggplant, okra, and peppers. Southern gardeners, though, have more problems. Here's a rundown of the most common pests and what can be done for them.

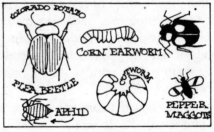

APHIDS

Small and of various colors, these sucking insects can drain the sap from eggplant, peppers, and okra all season long. If you notice ants near your plants, look for aphids. The aphids give off a sweet substance called "honeydew," which attracts the ants. Aphids also spread plant diseases, so be sure to control them if they're a problem. To get rid of aphids, try spraying with a mild solution of soapy water, or put out yellow pans of soapy water (aphids are attracted to yellow). If the infestation is severe, spray with an approved insecticide.

COLORADO POTATO BEETLES

These pests will feed on the foliage of eggplant and peppers. The adults are yellow with black stripes down their backs; larvae are reddish with a black head. Hand-pick adult beetles and larvae every time you see them. Crush egg masses under leaves. They can also be controlled by spraying with an approved insecticide.

CUTWORMS

These gray, brown, or black caterpillars chew tender transplants off at ground level. Cutworms are about one to one-and-a-half inches long and curl up tightly when disturbed. They hide in the soil and attack at night. You don't have to use anything to control them except newspaper cutworm collars at transplanting time (see page 33).

FLEA BEETLES

These tiny black or brown insects attack all three of these crops. They eat small holes in the leaves, usually early in the season, and if not controlled, can wipe out the foliage entirely, seriously injuring the plants. Dust with wood ashes or spray with a garlic or hot-pepper solution. Spraying with an approved insecticide will also control flea beetles.

PEPPER MAGGOTS

These insects infect peppers and can cause serious damage. The adults are yellow flies with brown bands on each wing. They lay their eggs within the peppers, and the maggots feed from the inside out. If you see any of the flies, spray with an approved insecticide to control them before they begin egg-laying.

PEPPER WEEVILS

These black-snouted beetles are very common in the South. They're only about ⅛ of an inch long. But don't let their size fool you; they can cause a great deal of damage. The adults feed on the foliage and lay eggs in the buds of immature pepper pods. The eggs hatch, and the larvae eat through the buds or fruit, causing them to drop or to be misshapen. To make matters worse, there may be several generations a year. An approved insecticide will help control them.

TOMATO FRUITWORM/CORN EARWORM

This is another pest of all three of these vegetables. Nearly 2 inches long, it is yellowish, green, or brown with lengthwise light and dark stripes. It bores into the pods or fruit, robbing you of good vegetables to put on your table. To control, hand-pick or spray with an approved insecticide at the first sign of damage.

Disease Problems

Eggplant, okra, and peppers are troubled by a few diseases, especially in the South. Since peppers and eggplant are related to tomatoes, they are susceptible to many tomato diseases as well as some of their own. There are some things a gardener can do to avoid them, though. As the old saying goes, "An ounce of prevention is worth a pound of cure." Follow these practices in the garden to avoid plant diseases.

Keep a close watch for insects, especially aphids. Plants that are weakened by insects are more susceptible to disease. Insects can also spread disease by carrying disease organisms on their bodies.

Weed your garden. Weeds can have diseases that can spread to your healthy plants. Weeds may also harbor disease-carrying insects. Mow around the garden if weeds are plentiful.

Stay out of the garden when it is wet. Diseases spread more rapidly among wet plants. If you are working among wet plants, disease organisms may cling to your clothes and find a new home in a drop of water on another plant. You could easily infect any plants that you brush against. Water during the early morning, so your plants have time to dry before nightfall. This helps check the spread of disease.

Plant disease-resistant varieties. Certain varieties of eggplant, okra, and peppers are resistant to wilts and other diseases. These varieties will be noted in the seed catalog or on the packet as being resistant.

Rotate your crops. Since some diseases are soil-borne, crop rotation will greatly reduce the chance of a crop being stricken year after year. Try not to plant any member of the same plant family in a spot where a member of that family has grown during the previous three years. This really cuts down on disease spread.

Garden sanitation. Removing all crop residue from the garden helps by eliminating debris which could carry disease organisms. You can compost the plant material you've removed, killing any disease agents present. This composted material can be added back to the garden soil.

It is helpful to identify the diseases affecting your crop. By following the appropriate controls you may be able to avoid further problems.

There are fungicides for controlling a few of the more serious diseases. Check with your extension service agent for currently recommended products.

Identifying Diseases

Disease	Appearance on Leaves, Stems, or Roots	Appearance on Fruit
Leaf spots	Small, yellowish-green or dark-brown spots on leaves. Water-soaked spots on old leaves.	Small, raised rough spots or rot spots. Fruit fails to set.
Anthracnose	Very little effect.	Dark circular sunken spots with pinkish to yellowish spores on peppers and eggplant.
Mosaic viruses	Green-yellow mottling of the leaf. Leaves become curved and irregular. Plant is usually stunted.	Yellow or wrinkled with dark spots. Small, bumpy, and off-colored.
Blossom end rot	No visible effect.	Big, black sunken ring on base of pepper.
Root knot nematodes	Produce galls (knots) on okra and pepper roots.	Stunted plants.
Wilts	Leaves wilt. Stunting and eventual death of plant.	Fruits are few, small, and of poor quality.
Phomopsis blight	Brown-to-gray circular spots on leaves and seedling stems of eggplant.	Brown-to-gray sunken spots that spread over entire eggplant fruit.

Source	Cultural Control
Seed-and-soil-borne fungi.	Use disease-free seed. Rotate plantings.
Seed. Soil. Infected plant debris.	Use disease-free seed. Do not cultivate when plants are wet. Rotate crops.
Aphids transmit the disease; humans may carry it from infected areas. Crop refuse.	Destroy infected plants. Do not use tobacco while handling. Wash hands with soap and water before handling. Control insects that transmit the disease. Use resistant varieties.
Lack of calcium. Dry spell following extra wet period.	Maintain pH 6.0–6.8. Use soils with high water-holding capacity. Mulch. Regular waterings.
Soil or seedling borne.	Rotate with grasses or legumes.
Soil.	Rotate crops.
Soil. Plant debris. Infected seed.	Rotate crops. Clean up plant debris at end of season.

HARVESTING

The most important thing about harvesting eggplant, peppers, and okra is to start as soon as there's something to eat. Since it's the job of the plant to make seeds, too much of the plant's effort goes into ripening the fruit instead of producing new fruit if you don't harvest regularly and often. So make it a practice to go out every few days and pick what's ready to eat. Try to get the most out of each plant. After all, having good things to eat is one of the main reasons to have a vegetable garden.

You can harvest peppers when they are as small as golfballs. Most peppers, except for a few varieties like

sweet banana peppers, are green when young. Don't be surprised if you see your bell peppers turning red; just about all of them do as they ripen. Harvest them by cutting through the stem of each fruit with a knife. You can have an almost continual harvest from your pepper plants by cutting often, because this encourages the plant to keep blossoming, especially in the beginning of the summer. Later in the season, leave some green peppers on your plants to turn red. They taste wonderful and are colorful in pepper relish.

Eggplant tastes best when harvested young. If you cut into an eggplant and find an abundance of brown seeds, it's already too late for good eating. The fruit will be a dark, glossy purple when it's ready to harvest. The surface of the eggplant turns dull and it will taste bitter as it gets older and past its prime. To harvest eggplant, cut through the stem above the green cap, or calyx, on the top. It's a tough stem, so have a sharp knife handy. The calyx also is a little prickly, so you may want to wear gloves to harvest eggplant.

Gloves and a long-sleeved shirt are practically a must when you harvest okra. The pods and leaves are usually covered with little spines that you can hardly see. These spines can get under your skin and make your hands and arms itch for days.

Okra grows so fast that you may have to harvest every day. A pod that is ready one day will be too tough to eat the next. The best pods, which are not more than 4 inches long, should be cut with a knife or broken right below the cap on the bottom. Since only one pod grows beneath each leaf, break off the leaf after harvesting the pod. This helps you remember where you've already harvested and indicates where to start the next time.

Okra plants grow so tall in the South that some people stand on ladders to harvest it. Okra doesn't get nearly that tall in the North. The tall stalks begin to look funny as the harvest progresses, and the leaves are taken off from the bottom up. When the plants get too tall to harvest, a southern gardener can cut the plant back about

12 to 18 inches above the ground. This is usually done in July or August. The plants will sprout again to make a second crop.

Stretching the Season

The best way to get the most out of your garden is to extend the harvest. There are a few ways to do this. If your growing season is long enough, you can make successive plantings about a week or so apart at the beginning of the season. Because you'll be harvesting at intervals, this method can be a big plus if you don't have the time to do all your canning, freezing, or pickling at once.

Another fun way to get a longer season from your peppers and eggplant is to bring your plants indoors. Bringing a few indoors when the outdoor gardening season is over gives you a double bonus for a while: more produce per plant and lush, green houseplants.

Before you attempt to bring your plants indoors, make sure they are healthy and that you have a good indoor location for them. They'll need a sunny window or fluorescent lights.

Up and In

Taking your plants from the garden requires the same care you took when you first transplanted them. The best time to do this is on a cloudy day or in the late afternoon. Have all your equipment ready beforehand. You'll need a garden spade, pots, and soil.

The pots should be deep enough to provide room for good root growth and their diameter should be about 10 to 14 inches. If you use old clay pots, scrub them well to

remove all traces of dirt and fertilizer salts (the white powdery stuff that collects on the inside of clay pots). Clay pots should be soaked in water overnight before you repot, to prevent the clay from absorbing the water you give the plants.

Any good brand of store-bought soil or sterilized garden soil lightened with peat moss, vermiculite, or perlite can be used as a potting mix.

Put a few stones or pieces of a broken clay pot in the bottom of the pot for drainage. Add a few inches of moist (not wet) potting mix and then thump the pot on the ground a few times to settle the soil.

Two hours before you plan to dig up your plants, give them a good soak. Take your garden spade and dig around the drip line of the leaves of your plant. It's a good idea to dig deeper than you think necessary, just to make sure you get the bulk of the roots. Dig straight down, not in toward the stem, to avoid cutting the roots. When you've dug deep enough, lift the plant out of the ground with a spade, supporting the stem with your hand. Gently place the plant in the pot. Fill in the spaces with potting mix, packing it in lightly around the roots. After shaking the pot to settle the soil and eliminate any air pockets, fill in any remaining space up to about an inch below the pot rim with the potting mix. Soak the plant until the water comes out of the drainage holes. Now your plant is ready to bring indoors.

Indoor Care

Indoor care is just about the same as outdoor care, but this time you have to play Mother Nature. Eggplant and pepper plants need a lot of light. They can be temperamental and may not produce if they don't like certain conditions, so keep them away from drafts, radiators, and heating ducts to avoid too cold or too hot a temperature.

Don't water them for a couple of days. This will give any broken roots a chance to heal and helps prevent root rot. After the first few days, keep them moist but not soaking wet.

Keep an eye out for insect pests, too. If you see the leaves starting to turn a splotchy yellow, look at the underside of the leaves. Whitish dusty grains are whitefly eggs or spider mite eggs. If you find them on the bottom of the leaves, it's time to act. If the plants are small enough,

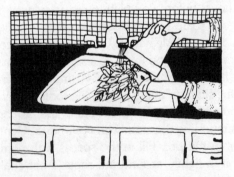

tip them upside down under a gentle spray of water and wash away the eggs.

If you use an insecticide, use one labeled for edible plants and use it only where you have proper ventilation and away from children and animals. Wait for a week or two after spraying before harvesting, and wash the fruit before you eat it.

Since the eggplant and pepper plants grown inside don't have all the benefits of full sunshine, the fruit is not as large as fruit grown outdoors. The indoor fruits are usually one-third to one-half as large as the outdoor ones. But since nothing beats eating garden-fresh vegetables, they're worth it.

After you've enjoyed your plants for a few months, they'll start to look peaked. Pick off the fruit and compost the plants. You've gotten your money's worth.

Bees Do It—But Only Outdoors

Bees provide pollination for your plants outside. Indoors, you're in charge. When your plants are in bloom, take a cotton swab or a fine paintbrush (the kind you might use for watercolors) and transfer the pollen from one flower to another. Just swirl the swab or brush lightly inside each flower, one after the other. Repeat this process again on the next day to make sure you catch the flowers when they're ready.

Not all of them will produce fruit. Where you have met with success, you will be able to see tiny fruits as the flowers wilt. Don't wait too long after the blossoms appear to pollinate, or they'll wilt before you have a chance. Do your "bee act" within a day after the blossoms open.

GENERAL COOKING TIPS

Eggplant

Eggplant is both beautiful and versatile. The dark-purple skin and bright green stem on this vegetable encloses the meaty pulp—a low-calorie, low-fat food that deserves more attention. The trouble is that it's fairly new to many gardeners in this country, who sometimes avoid cooking it because they simply don't know more than one recipe. Finding new ways to serve eggplant is a lot like experimenting with summer squash; once you start, the possibilities really open up.

There's no need to peel eggplant; the skin is perfectly edible when cooked.

Many cooks prefer to remove the moisture from sliced eggplant before cooking, so the dish isn't overly watery. There are a few ways to do this. You can pat and drain slices thoroughly between paper towels with fairly good results, or salt slices liberally to draw out water, then drain them on wire racks. Another method is to stack slices, cover them with a plate, and place a heavy weight on top to squeeze out excess moisture.

Like so many light-fleshed vegetables, eggplant discolors when it's cut open. You can prevent this by sprinkling or rubbing the slices with lemon juice as soon as you cut them. Or dilute 3 Tablespoons of lemon juice in a large bowl of water and place each eggplant slice in this "antidarkening" solution until you're ready to cook it. It also helps to use stainless steel knives and noncorrosive cookware such as stainless steel, glass, or enamel.

Eggplant can be steamed, sautéed, fried, baked, or combined with many other foods in casseroles or vegetable medleys.

Okra

This southern specialty is a good source of vitamins A and C. It can be served alone or in soups or stews. Okra is delicious served with melted butter and a squeeze of lemon or dipped in an egg batter and deep-fried. Another name for okra is gumbo; that's why soups containing okra are often called gumbos. These thick and hearty soups usually include meat, fish, chicken, and other vegetables. The okra, a natural thickening agent, is used instead of flour or other starch.

To cook, wash the pods well and cut off stem ends. Cut in ½-inch slices and cook in boiling salted water ten to fifteen minutes, or until just tender.

Okra will keep well for a few days in your refrigerator in a covered container, or you can easily freeze or can it.

Peppers

Raw or cooked, sweet peppers are delicious. Serve them in salads. soups, stews, snacks, cut in rings as a garnish, in casseroles, or stuffed and baked as a main dish. Since they're so easy to freeze, you can depend on a year-round supply from just one gardening season.

Red and green peppers are good sources of vitamin C, some vitamin A, and small amounts of several beneficial minerals. Red peppers contain more vitamin A and C than green ones, and raw peppers are richer in vitamins than cooked ones.

You don't need exact recipes to get the most from your pepper crop. Sauté whole sweet banana peppers (stems, seeds, and all) in a few Tablespoons of butter or oil for a quick, delicious side dish. Sliced peppers and onions sautéed with home-fried potatoes go great together for a quick, colorful side dish. Or, add cooked, chopped peppers to scrambled eggs for an instant western omelet. To roast peppers, brush them lightly with oil and bake or broil until browned.

Drying Peppers

In addition to canning and freezing peppers, you can grow your own "spice" peppers to dry for use all year long. Just plant the variety you want, let the fruit turn red on the plant, and harvest.

Harvest the entire plant in late summer and dry by hanging the plants upside down in a warm, well-ventilated spot. Peppers can also be dried off the plants. Dried peppers will keep for two years or more in a dry place.

You can also string peppers with a needle on strong thread. Keep them in a cool, dry, dark place until they are totally dry, and then hang the ropes of dried peppers where it's warm and dry. Dried peppers are great for seasoning sauces or concocting a special supper.

The Spice Rack

Peppers are truly multipurpose vegetables, since certain varieties are used to make seasonings and spices. Paprika, cayenne pepper, chili powder, and Tabasco sauce are all made from various kinds of peppers.

If you want to make your own spices, simply remove the stems and seeds from dried peppers. Grind the peppers to the consistency you want. Chili pepper flakes are a convenient size for seasoning sauces, chilies, stews, and Mexican dishes. Store the ground peppers in airtight containers.

Be careful about the quantity of these hot peppers you use in recipes. A whole one is often too much!

If you're looking for another way to use hot peppers, try making a spicy vinegar. Combine twenty-four red chili peppers in a quart of distilled white vinegar and cover tightly. Shake the contents daily. After two weeks, strain the vinegar and place in a tightly corked jar. Use this homemade vinegar for your "house" French or Italian dressing. To make a milder vinegar, use fewer peppers. Add salt or other seasonings according to taste.

You can also preserve long, thin, red chili peppers in sherry, for an unusual salad or hors d'oeuvres ingredient. Just pack the peppers into sterile jars, add the sherry, cover, and store in a cool, dark place. The peppers will keep indefinitely. Add more sherry or peppers as needed to keep the jars full.

FAVORITE RECIPES

RATATOUILLE

This classic French dish may be difficult to pronounce, but it's easy to make and it's one of our very favorite garden recipes. Feel free to use more or less of each ingredient—the amounts don't have to be precise for a delicious result.

  1 medium onion, chopped fine
  2 cloves garlic, peeled and crushed
  ⅓ cup olive oil
  1 large eggplant, peeled and cubed
  2 medium zucchini, sliced in ½-inch pieces (don't peel)
1–2 medium peppers, cut in strips
  6 ripe, medium-size tomatoes, quartered (or 2 cups canned tomatoes)
    basil
    salt and pepper

In large skillet or saucepan, sauté onion and garlic in oil until onion is transparent. Stir in remaining vegetables; add basil, salt, and pepper to taste. Simmer, covered, over low heat for thirty minutes. Uncover and simmer fifteen minutes more, or until liquid is reduced and mixture has thickened slightly. Serve this as a hot or cold side dish. Serves 6 to 8.

EGGPLANT DIP

*T*his is a garden-fresh dip that goes well with raw vegetables or crackers.

1 eggplant
¼ cup chopped onion
1 Tbsp chopped chives or scallions
½ cup chopped tomatoes
¼ cup chopped celery
¼ cup chopped red or green pepper
2 cloves garlic, minced
2 tsp lemon juice
¼ cup sour cream or plain yogurt
½ cup mayonnaise
  salt and pepper to taste.

Optional:
1 Tbsp horseradish sauce for added zip
  paprika as garnish

Place eggplant in a large kettle, cover with water, and bring to a boil. Cook until soft, about twenty-five minutes. Dip in cold water to cool. Peel and chop into a bowl. Add all remaining ingredients. Mix well. If you prefer a finer texture, blend all ingredients in a blender or food processor until smooth. Chill at least two hours. Garnish with sprinkle of paprika before serving. Makes about 3 cups.

EGGPLANT-SPAGHETTI BAKE

This is quick and simple, with no frying needed. For large gatherings, simply double the recipe and bake it in two pans.

½ cup bread crumbs
¾ cup grated Parmesan cheese
1 large eggplant
¼ cup mayonnaise
1 8-oz package spaghetti
2 Tbsp margarine
1 lb ground beef
6 cups thick spaghetti sauce
8 oz mozzarella cheese

Preheat oven to 425°F. Combine bread crumbs and ¼ cup of the Parmesan cheese in a shallow dish. Wash and cut eggplant into ½-inch slices.

Spread mayonnaise sparingly on both sides of each eggplant slice. Dip slices in crumb mixture to coat both sides, then place on an ungreased cookie sheet. Bake for about fifteen minutes, until browned and tender. Remove from oven and lower temperature to 375°F.

Cook spaghetti according to directions on package. Drain and toss with margarine until spaghetti is coated. Cover spaghetti and keep warm. Crumble beef in a skillet and brown over low heat. Add spaghetti sauce and heat through.

Grease a 13″ × 9″ baking dish. Pour one cup of sauce in the bottom of the pan, then place spaghetti on top. Pour remaining sauce over spaghetti. Arrange slices of eggplant over the spaghetti, then top with strips of mozzarella cheese.

Bake fifteen minutes or until it is heated through and the mozzarella cheese is melted. Sprinkle remaining Parmesan cheese on top. Serves 6 to 8.

EGGPLANT AND RICE PATTIES

   2 cups peeled, cooked, mashed eggplant
1½ cups cooked rice, cooled
   2 eggs, slightly beaten
   1 cup shredded cheddar cheese
   1 Tbsp grated onion
   ¼ cup cornmeal or 2 Tbsp flour
   1 tsp salt
   2 drops Tabasco sauce (use more if you like it hot)
   ½ cup salad oil

Combine all the ingredients except oil. Mix well. Form into patties. Place in skillet with oil, heated to 375°F. Cook until brown on both sides. Drain on paper towels. Makes about 18 patties.

GREEK MOUSSAKA

A delicious eggplant casserole.

2 large eggplants
olive oil
2 cloves garlic, minced
2 onions, chopped
1 lb ground lamb (or ground beef)
2 Tbsp tomato paste
½ cup red wine
¼ cup chopped parsley
½ tsp oregano
1 tsp cinnamon
1 tsp sugar
salt and pepper to taste
½ cup fine bread crumbs
¼ cup butter or margarine
2 cups milk
⅛ tsp grated nutmeg
2 eggs slightly beaten
½ cup grated Parmesan cheese

Slice unpeeled eggplants into ¼-inch rounds, and in a large skillet lightly sauté a few slices at a time in olive oil. Set aside.

Add more olive oil to skillet if needed and sauté the garlic, onion, and ground lamb until the lamb is browned. Stir in tomato paste, wine, parsley, oregano, cinnamon, sugar, salt, and pepper, and simmer until the liquid has nearly evaporated. Stir in bread crumbs.

Place a layer of eggplant slices in the bottom of a deep

casserole dish, then spread a layer of meat sauce. Alternate layers of eggplant and sauce until ingredients are all used, ending with a layer of eggplant.

In a saucepan, melt margarine. Add milk and nutmeg and heat for two to three minutes. Remove from heat, add eggs, and mix well. Pour custard mixture over casserole, allowing it to penetrate sides and lower layers. Sprinkle cheese on top and bake 35 to 40 minutes in 350°F oven. Serves 4 to 6.

DEEP-FRIED EGGPLANT

    1 large eggplant, washed, peeled, and cut into
       ½-inch strips
1½ tsp salt
    1 cup flour
    2 eggs, slightly beaten
    1 cup milk
    1 Tbsp salad oil
       hot oil (salad)

To prepare eggplant for frying, sprinkle eggplant with 1 tsp of the salt, cover with water, and soak one hour. Drain, then pat dry with paper towels.

In a mixing bowl, combine flour, ½ tsp salt, eggs, milk, and 1 Tbsp salad oil. Beat until smooth.

Dip eggplant strips in batter and deep-fry in hot oil until medium brown. Drain on paper towels. Serves 4 to 6.

SHRIMP-STUFFED EGGPLANT

2 medium-size eggplant
½ cup chopped scallions
½ cup chopped celery
2 cloves garlic, minced
2 Tbsp margarine, melted
6 slices bread
1 cup water
¼ cup parsley flakes
½ tsp salt
⅛ tsp black pepper
⅛ tsp cayenne
2 4½-oz cans tiny shrimp, drained
2 eggs, beaten
3 cups spaghetti sauce
¼ cup grated Parmesan cheese

Cook eggplant in boiling water for fifteen minutes. Drain and let cool. Cut in half lengthwise. Scoop out pulp, leaving shells intact. Chop pulp and reserve.

Sauté scallions, celery, and garlic in margarine until tender. Soak bread in water, then drain and squeeze out water. Add bread, parsley, pulp, salt, pepper, cayenne, and shrimp to scallion mix. Stir. Cool slightly. Add eggs and mix well.

Place eggplant shells in a greased baking dish; fill each with shrimp mixture. Spoon spaghetti sauce over each eggplant. Sprinkle with cheese. Bake at 400°F 20 to 25 minutes. To serve, cut each shell in half. Serves 8.

STOVE-TOP EGGPLANT PARMIGIANA

1 eggplant, cut into ¼-inch slices
½ cup milk
½ tsp salt
¼ tsp pepper
1 cup fine bread crumbs
  salad oil
2 cups tomato sauce
16 oz mozzarella cheese, shredded
¼ cup grated Parmesan cheese

Dip eggplant slices in milk, salt, and pepper, then coat both sides with bread crumbs. Heat 2 Tbsp oil and sauté eggplant slices in a large skillet over medium heat until tender and browned on both sides. Add more oil as needed. When browned, remove slices to a plate.

When all eggplant slices are browned, pour ⅔ cup of the tomato sauce in the bottom of the skillet; layer half of the eggplant slices on the sauce. Sprinkle half of the mozzarella cheese over eggplant. Repeat with another layer of each. Heat over medium-high heat until boiling. Reduce heat to low and simmer ten to fifteen minutes, until heated through. Sprinkle with Parmesan cheese and serve. Serves 4 to 6.

This recipe may also be layered in a casserole or baking dish and baked in a 350°F oven for thirty minutes.

COLORFUL OKRA DISH

Fresh okra, corn off the cob, and ripe tomatoes make this easy side dish delicious. Make it as a surprise for your next company meal.

2½ cups sliced okra
1½ cups fresh corn, cut off cob
  4 large tomatoes, chopped
 ¼ cup chopped onion
 ¼ cup margarine, melted
    salt and pepper to taste

  Wash and slice okra, rinse well under running water, and drain.
  Combine okra with remaining ingredients in large skillet, cover, and simmer for fifteen minutes. Serves 6.

PICKLED DILL OKRA

2½ quarts young okra
 3 celery leaves (for each pint)
 1 clove garlic (for each pint)
 1 large head dill and stem (for each pint)
 3 cups water
1½ cups white vinegar
 ¼ cup salt

Scrub okra, then pack whole pods in hot pint jars. In each jar place 3 celery leaves, 1 clove peeled garlic, and 1 head and stem of dill. Bring water, vinegar, and salt to a boil. Pour the boiling liquid over the okra and seal jars. Process five minutes in a hot water bath.

For best pickle flavor, let stand four weeks before eating. Makes 4 pints.

OKRA FRITTERS

1 cup flour
2 tsp baking powder
1 tsp salt
⅛ tsp pepper
2 eggs, beaten
1 tsp onion, minced
1 Tbsp margarine, melted
1 cup milk
2 cups sliced okra (¼-inch strips), cooked and drained
½ cup salad oil

Combine dry ingredients, stir in eggs, onion, margarine and milk. Fold okra into batter and mix lightly.

Drop batter by tablespoons into skillet or fryer with 375°F heated oil. Cook two minutes on each side, or until lightly browned. Drain on paper towels. Makes 16 fritters.

OKRA BEEF SUPPER

1 lb ground beef
¾ cups chopped onion
1 garlic clove, minced
4 cups canned tomatoes
½ cup uncooked rice
¼ cup bread crumbs
1 tsp salt
⅛ tsp pepper
6 drops Tabasco sauce
2 cups sliced okra

Brown ground beef, onion, and garlic in skillet. Add tomatoes and simmer. Add remaining ingredients, except okra. Cover and simmer for twenty minutes.

Stir in okra, cover, and simmer again until rice is done (twenty to twenty-five minutes). Stir occasionally. Serves 6 to 8.

NORTH-SOUTH GUMBO

6 strips bacon
3 cups sliced okra
1 cup diced celery
1 green pepper, chopped
1 medium onion, chopped
2 cups corn
1 cup diced potatoes
6 large fresh tomatoes, chopped (or 4 cups canned
   tomatoes)
2 cups flaked cooked fish
2 tsp brown sugar
¼ tsp paprika
4 cups water
   salt and pepper to taste

Cut bacon in small pieces, place in skillet and sauté with okra, celery, green pepper, and onion for five minutes.

Combine all ingredients in a large kettle and simmer for one hour. Serve hot. Serves 6.

GREEN PEPPER JELLY

This is delicious served with lamb or pork.

7 medium green peppers, washed, seeded, cored, and cut in pieces.
1½ cups vinegar
2 hot red peppers, washed, cored, seeded, and diced
3–6 cups sugar
½ tsp salt
1 bottle liquid pectin

Put half the green peppers and half the vinegar in a blender and liquefy. Pour into large kettle. Place remaining peppers and vinegar in blender and liquefy. Add to kettle and stir in red peppers, sugar, and salt.

Bring to a boil and add pectin. Boil until mixture thickens when dropped from spoon—about twenty minutes. Skim off foam. Pour into clean, hot half-pint canning jars.

Fill jars quickly to within ⅛ inch of top. Wipe jar rims and threads with a clean, damp cloth. Put on hot lids and screw band on tightly. Process in a boiling water bath for ten minutes. Cool, then test to be sure a seal has formed. Store jars in a cool, dry place. Makes about 4 half-pints.

PEPPER RELISH

This is a favorite hot dog relish. It's a must at any "wiener roast."

12 green sweet peppers, finely chopped (8 cups)
12 red sweet peppers, finely chopped (8 cups)
 1 hot pepper, finely chopped
 3 cups finely chopped onions
 2 cups vinegar
 1 cup sugar
 1 Tbsp salt
 1 Tbsp mixed pickling spices

Place chopped peppers and onions in large kettle. Cover with boiling water and let stand five minutes. Drain. Cover again with boiling water and let stand ten minutes; drain.

Simmer vinegar, sugar, salt, and spices (tied in a bag) fifteen minutes. Add drained vegetables and simmer ten minutes. Remove spice bag. Bring relish to a boil and pour into hot jars, leaving ¼ inch headspace. Adjust lids. Process ten minutes in boiling water bath. Makes about 6 half pints.

PICKLED PEPPERS

8 quarts peppers

Pickling liquid:
¼ cup sugar
8 cups vinegar
2 cups water
2 cloves garlic (per jar)

Use red, green, yellow banana, cherry, or hot peppers. Hot peppers can be "cooled" to your taste by adding sweet peppers to them. For lively color, mix red, green, and yellow in some jars.

Wash peppers. (Remember to wear rubber gloves when washing and handling hot peppers, to prevent your hands from burning.)

If using small whole peppers, cut two small slits in each pepper to allow for complete pickling. When using larger peppers, cut stems off, take out seeds, and cut in fourths or eighths. Cut in squares, they're the perfect "cracker" size for hors d'oeuvres.

Combine all ingredients except garlic in a kettle; simmer for fifteen minutes.

Pack peppers and garlic into hot jars, leaving ¼ inch headspace. For a little extra zip, add 1 whole hot pepper to each jar of sweet peppers. Heat pickling liquid to boiling, pour over peppers, leaving ¼ inch headspace. Adjust caps. Process pints for ten minutes in boiling water bath.

Makes about 8 pints.

PEPPER SLAW

3 sweet green peppers
3 sweet red peppers
3 large onions
1 head cabbage
1 Tbsp salt
1½ cups sugar
2 tsp celery seeds
2 tsp mustard seeds
  vinegar

Wash and core peppers and remove seeds. Coarsely chop peppers, onions, and cabbage. Add salt, mix, and let stand in refrigerator overnight. Drain the liquid formed by mixture. Add sugar and spices and mix well. Cover with vinegar and bring to a boil, then boil for twenty to twenty-five minutes. Cool and refrigerate. Makes about 7 cups.

This recipe can be doubled and canned. All you need to do after boiling for fifteen to thirty minutes is pour into hot pint jars, leaving ½ inch headspace; adjust lids.

Process in a boiling water bath for five minutes. Makes 7 pints.

PORK-STUFFED PEPPER WEDGES

1 lb ground lean pork, cooked
⅓ cup chopped celery
¼ cup chopped, canned mushrooms
¼ cup chopped green onions
2 Tbsp soy sauce
4 large green or red peppers cut in quarters
  cooked green peas for garnish (optional)

Combine pork, celery, mushrooms, and onions in a bowl. Mix, then add soy sauce.

Stuff pepper quarters. Garnish each pepper with a few peas. Steam or bake in 350°F oven for fifteen minutes. Serve with additional soy sauce and rice. Serves 6 to 8.

MEXICAN OMELET

Here's a hot and tangy quiche, without the crust. It's perfect for a Sunday brunch.

¼ lb bacon
½ diced onion
1 green pepper, cored and diced
12 eggs
½ cup milk
1 tsp minced hot chili pepper
  salt and pepper to taste
  dash curry powder
½ cup sharp cheddar cheese, grated

Cook bacon until crisp. Drain bacon and pour off all but 2 Tbsp bacon fat. Sauté onion and green pepper in bacon fat until onion is translucent. Beat eggs in a large bowl. Stir in milk, chili pepper, salt, pepper, and curry powder, and pour into a greased oblong or round baking dish. Top with onions, peppers, crumbled bacon, and cheese. Bake in 350°F oven for twenty-five minutes, or until eggs are set and the top is slightly brown. Serves 4 to 6.

ITALIAN-STYLE PIMIENTOS

1. Preheat oven to 400°F. Wash 6 to 10 red pimiento peppers. Leave whole and place on an ungreased cookie sheet. Roast for thirty minutes, turning and browning each side until the pepper skins are charred.

2. Remove from oven and place peppers—cookie sheet and all—in a large paper bag to cool. This keeps the peppers from becoming soft. When cool, remove peppers from paper bag, slip skins off peppers, core, and remove seeds. Do this over a bowl to catch juices that run out of peppers. Still over the bowl, tear peppers into ½-inch strips. (Tearing is easier than using a knife to cut.) Reserve pepper liquid in bowl.

3. To help peppers keep their shape, layer strips in small freezer containers. Place one leaf of fresh basil in each container and pour reserved liquid over the top. Pimientos can be frozen at this point for year-round use.

4. To prepare for serving, thaw pimientos and cover with Italian marinade: olive oil to cover, 1 garlic clove cut in half, 1 tsp oregano, salt and pepper to taste. Refrigerate marinated peppers for one to two hours to allow flavors to blend. They'll keep in the refrigerator for a few weeks.

These peppers are an important antipasto ingredient. They are also delicious in Italian grinders or served with tuna salad.

Eggplant

The most successful way to freeze eggplant is in precooked casseroles or Italian dishes. But if you have a large harvest or you want to freeze some slices to have on hand for frying, you can freeze it without too much trouble.

Pick eggplant when skins are a dark color all over. Prepare enough for one scalding at a time and work quickly, since eggplant discolors. Wash, peel, and slice ½-inch thick, or cut ½- to 1-inch cubes.

Scald four minutes in 1 gallon boiling water with ½ cup lemon juice or 4½ tsp citric acid. Eggplant can also be dropped in 1 gallon cold water and ½ cup salt to prevent darkening. Cool, drain, and place in freezer containers leaving ½ inch headspace. Slices may be separated by sheets of freezer paper, then put into containers. Seal, label, date, and freeze.

Okra

Use 2-to-3½-inch green pods. Wash, cut off stems but do not cut the pods open. Blanch three minutes. Drain and cool quickly in cold water. Drain and leave whole or slice. Pack in containers leaving ½ inch headspace. Seal, label, date, and freeze.

Peppers

By freezing part of the summer's harvest, you can save money and add flavor to winter sauces and dishes. You can take just a few pieces of frozen peppers for a dish, and the remainder in the container stays nicely frozen. Peppers are a snap to freeze because they don't have to be blanched. Choose firm, crisp, red or green thick-walled peppers. Wash, cut out stems, and remove seeds. Cut peppers in halves, rings or strips, or dice. Pack into freezer containers, leaving no headspace. Seal, label, date, and freeze. Use unblanched frozen peppers just as you would fresh.

Peppers freeze perfectly well whole, but since they take up so much room in the freezer, you may prefer to freeze halves for stuffing. If you want to fit more peppers into each freezer container, blanch them for a few minutes to make them limp. Blanch halves for three minutes, slices for two minutes. Cool in cold water; drain well. Pack in freezer containers, leaving ½ inch headspace for blanched peppers. Seal, label, date, and freeze. Use scalded peppers in recipes that call for cooked peppers. You don't have to thaw them; just add to soups, casseroles, or tomato sauce.

CANNING

Canning isn't usually the first choice of a way to preserve these vegetables, because freezing and pickling work so well. However, eggplant can be pressure-canned to have available for a quick dish or relish, eggplant patties, or ratatouille. Pressure-canning peppers and okra is a good way to preserve them if you don't have a freezer.

Because eggplant, okra, and peppers are low-acid vegetables, they must be canned under pressure unless you make them into relish or pickle them.

For more information on basic canning procedures, contact your local county extension service office.

About the
National Gardening Association

The National Gardening Association is a nonprofit member-supported organization dedicated to helping people be successful gardeners at home, in community groups, and in institutions. We believe gardening adds joy and health to living, while improving the environment and encouraging an appreciation for the proper stewardship of the earth.

Established in 1972, this national organization of 250,000 members is now the premier membership organization for gardeners.

Members receive the monthly *National Gardening* magazine, may write the staff horticulturist for help with any gardening problem, receive discounts on gardening books, and get other member benefits. *National Gardening* magazine provides in-depth, how-to articles, profiles of members and their gardens, and evaluations of garden tools and products. Regional articles help members with special climate challenges. The magazine also provides a forum for NGA members in a "Seed Swap" exchange column, and seed and recipe search columns.

The National Gardening Association is a nationwide resource for information, services, and publications related to gardening. Besides the monthly magazine, NGA produces numerous books and directories for the home gardener. NGA also produces the annual *National Gardening Survey*, from research conducted for NGA by the Gallup Organization. This comprehensive report on trends in home gardening in America is widely used by the lawn and garden industry and is cited by the nation's media.

Well known as the information clearinghouse for community garden programs across the country, NGA offers on-site planning assistance, specialized manuals, a network to other organizations, and the annual National Gardening Grant Program—for gardens in neighborhoods, schools, and institutions, especially garden groups for youth, senior citizens, and people with disabilities.

The National Gardening Association continues to explore new ways to gather and share information, to connect gardeners with other gardeners, and to further its mission—successful gardeners everywhere!

If you would like a free sample issue of the *National Gardening* magazine and information on member benefits and how to join the National Gardening Association, please write or call:

The National Gardening Association
180 Flynn Avenue
Burlington, Vermont 05401
(802) 863-1308

Villard's National Gardening Association Series

☐ 75000-4
BOOK OF TOMATOES
$4.95;
in Canada, $7.50

☐ 74991-X
BOOK OF LETTUCE & GREENS
$4.95;
in Canada, $7.50

☐ 74990-1
BOOK OF EGGPLANT, OKRA & PEPPERS
$4.95;
in Canada, $7.50

☐ 74988-X
BOOK OF CUCUMBERS, MELONS & SQUASH
$4.95;
in Canada, $7.50

To order, send check or money order (no cash or CODs) to:

Villard Books, c/o Random House, Inc., 400 Hahn Road, Westminster, MD 21157

Please enclose $1.00 for the first book and 50¢ for each additional book to cover postage and handling. Make checks payable to Villard Books. If you have a major credit card, you can charge by phone by calling:
(800) 638-6460

You may also charge to your credit card by mailing in this coupon.

Please send me the books I have checked above.

NAME (please print)

ADDRESS

CITY/STATE   ZIP

PLEASE CHECK ONE: MASTERCARD ☐   VISA ☐
                                  AMERICAN EXPRESS ☐

CARD NUMBER

EXPIRATION DATE

SIGNATURE

Please add applicable sales tax. Allow 4–6 weeks for delivery.